You So Pretty

By Wonda Thomas

To: Heddie

Wonda Thomas
3-26-21
Be Blessed

Copyright © 2021 Wonda Thomas

Copyright © 2021 Lady Knight Enterprises Publishing

Duluth, Georgia

www.ladyknightenterprisespublishing.com

All rights reserved. No part of this publication, contents and/or cover may be reproduced in whole or in part in any form without the express, written permission of the Author or Publisher. This includes stored in a retrieval system, or transmitted in any form or means, for example but not limited to; photocopying, recording, electronic copying, mechanical, scanning, or otherwise. It is illegal to copy this book, post it to a website, or distribute it by any other means without written permission from the Author or Publisher.

Printed in the United States of America.

YOU SO PRETTY

All rights reserved.

ISBN: 978-1-7358663-3-8

(Lady Knight Enterprises Publishing)

Cover artwork created by Connie Blackmon

DEDICATION

I would like to dedicate this book to all the women and men who have been misused, mistreated, and thought the only way to receive love was through sex. Also, to the ones that had their innocence taken and just did not know what was going on, like myself. I pray this book helps you and heals your heart. You will overcome it! Give it to God, forgive, release, and try to put it behind you. Always remember, regardless of what you go through in life, or in relationships, just know within yourself 'YOU SO PRETTY.' Nobody has to tell you that, or lie to you, just to get you to do things you don't feel comfortable with.

CONTENTS

	Acknowledgments	I
	Introduction	1
1	THE BEGINNING	2
2	INNOCENT	4
3	THE UNEXPECTED	8
4	FIRST LOVE	11
5	PARTY LIFE	16
6	TRAPPED	20
7	GROWTH	22
8	AM I THE ONE?	27
9	THE ENGAGEMENT	29
10	THE FINAL STRAW	33
11	MAD	36
12	THE REMIX	43
13	THE BLESSING	49
14	LESSONS & CONSEQUENCES	54

ACKNOWLEDGMENTS

I cannot express enough thanks to my support team for their continued support and encouragements: My Mother, Melsnease Renderand and Apostles Melvin & Jacqualine Cartwright, for continued prayers for my children, and myself, throughout my youth and adult life; and Mentor, Lonzie Tramble. I offer my sincere appreciation for the learning opportunities provided. Your encouragement when the times got rough, are much appreciated and duly noted. I love you all so much.

INTRODUCTION

Secretly, every day, for a year, I beat myself up. I was mad with myself. I was at church one day and ran out crying. I didn't know someone came right behind me. She stood with me and let me cry it out. I told her everything that happened, from the beginning to the end. I was still angry with the dad. She said, "You have to forgive him." I said, "No! I'm not ready. He did something to me that I didn't ask for, and I'm mad."

I've seen so many nasty men who love young girls, will have sex with them, and don't care. I think about things I've been through in my life. It just makes me cry. If only you could be a fly on my wall.

CHAPTER 1

THE BEGINNING

It all started when a little, pretty, chocolate 19 year-old met this handsome, milk chocolate 17 year-old in 1979. My mom, who was a country girl, had moved from this little country town of Lafayette, AL., to the little city of Lanett, AL. My grandmother, my mom, and her 6 siblings moved to the housing projects in Lanett. I call this the beginning because it is where my mom and dad met.

I asked my dad how he met my mom? He said, "That little pretty, black girl used to be fixing hair, and I would go where she was. She was new in town and I liked her." My dad said she just was so pretty with her chocolate self.

I asked my mom what she thought about my dad and she said, "That man know he was fine and was looking good to me." These two dated and eventually, I had a brother. My mom told me he was stillborn. He was so small; she could hold him in her hand.

May 1980, I entered the world. Since my brother did not survive, I was my dad's only child. I know that had to be exciting for him. My mom already had a 5-year-old daughter from a previous marriage, when I was born. I often wished my brother would have made it and I would have had a big brother too, but then, I thought about if he had lived, my parents probably wouldn't have wanted anymore kids. My dad and mom eventually split, and he got married.

My mom tells me to this day, that my dad was the best dad to me. She said, "I didn't have to make him do anything. He took care of you and spent time with you." My stepmom and dad had twin girls. I'm two years older than them, but she was good to me. She treated me like her own. She never made a difference between me and my twin sisters.

I used to go over their house, a lot. My dad had one issue that I won't speak on, however, it never affected me. He was still the best dad to me and was very much active in my life.

He always came to get me, and made sure he took me around my siblings, and my family, on his side. If I got in trouble or got out of hand, my mom would call my dad, and he would come, with no hesitation. My mom and my dad co-parented and had no issues. They were the best parents and did what they had to do to take care of me.

I'm a grown woman, but still my dad often tells me when we talk, he's so proud of me. He always says, "You're my first baby, and you don't depend on nobody." My mom always tells me she's so proud of me as well, even though I was very rebellious as a teen. I turned out to be a wonderful woman and mother, all because of them.

They just didn't know in 1980, that their pretty, little baby girl that they brought into this world, would have to endure so much hurt and pain in life, all because she would grow up to be SO PRETTY!!!

CHAPTER 2

INNOCENT

When I think back on being a very small, little girl, I remember being over my aunt's house. I was about 6 or 7. I remember being in a room, with some older boys. I can't recall what I was doing, except being a child, but I remember those boys trying to put their finger inside of me. I remember hearing, "It won't go. I need some Vaseline." I knew something was wrong in my little mind, but I was a little girl, what was I to do? I didn't even know what to think at all.

I never said anything to anyone, because I was so little, and I didn't know it was wrong. That only happened once. Even as a little girl, I knew all of them well. Now, one of them is deceased. He was killed some years back, and the others are still around. They may not even remember what they did, but I sure do.

I didn't know anything about boys, I only knew to play. I even had a cousin who always wanted me to come outside, when I was over my grandmother's house, and would rub my vagina. I thought it was normal, so I went. I was only 8 then. It makes you wonder, why would my boy cousin want to rub in his little cousin's vagina, every time I went over, and he was there? I have heard through different conversations, that I wasn't the only one he was rubbing on in the family. Very, very sad huh?

A few years later, I was around the age of 10 and still playing like 10 year-olds would, with their siblings and cousins. I loved to play and play with them! One night I went to bed trying to sleep, and my cousin said, "Let me show you something." I said, "Okay." I didn't know what was going to happen. She would say "Pull your panties down." What!!!

"I've got to show you something." I felt a few strokes of her tongue on my vagina. I asked, "What are you doing?!" Instantly I said, "Who showed you this? Who have you been watching?" I believed it was Ann's parents because that was unusual for her. It happened on several occasions, every time I went to my aunts, to the point, I expected it. It was weird and strange that my cousin wanted to do this to me but, I was a child and I didn't really understand.

Sometimes my aunt would come check on us and Ann would just tell me to "Act like you're sleep." Of course, I did, and she would go right back between my legs, putting her tongue on my vagina, once my aunt closed the door. It was weird! We played throughout the day like we would normally do, but at night, she always wanted to go between my legs.

That eventually stopped after a few years because my mom started her own business, so we were able to stay home and didn't have to be at anyone else's house. We were getting older and could stay home until she got off work.

As time went by, I didn't think about all those things that happened to me. I tried to live a normal life as a teen, even though the experiences with what my family members did to me was very nasty and not normal. I was still boy crazy, maybe because of what happened to me. I thought I had to do things for boys to like me. The main words I always heard were, "you so pretty!" Did I sleep with boys then? Nooo! But, if I liked you, and was in a relationship with you, it was a thought.

By the time I reached middle school, I used to be in school, hearing girls talking about sex, at the age of 12, and what they were doing with these boys. I used to say, "my mom would beat me if I did that." Some of the girls were pregnant and talking about a boyfriend at that age. I couldn't even wear lipstick then, and they got boyfriends and were having sex.

The things that had happened to me, I guess I pushed them so far behind in my head that I forgot about it, to a certain extent, but I never fully forgot.

I started going to parties and clubs at the age of 13. Oh, I was in another world then. I think I just used to like to get out of the house, because my mother was so strict. I couldn't even talk on the phone without her listening. I used to be so embarrassed because she would say, "Get off this phone;" in the middle of my conversation. I would be so mad. It's funny now, but now I realize it was for my good.

Now, let me explain something to you, I had a wonderful mother! She was a little strict, but she raised her kids to be respectful. We were taught to say, no ma'am and yes ma'am. If adults were talking, we had to say excuse me, then get permission to say what we had to say and go on out of the room, after we asked a question. My Mother always kept us in church. It was four of us. She didn't play the radio either. It was just her and us four kids, until she got married, when I was a teen. My mom worked, went to sleep, and we went to church.

I remember when I was a small child, we would go to this restaurant called Bonanza, in Columbus, GA. I was so ready to see those thick black plates with the metal on the bottom, every Sunday after church. I used to be so excited! I have forgotten what we used to eat, but it was just the excitement of going.

My Mother doesn't know it, but she was a good example and role model to me. I watched her work and take care of us. I watched her do things around the house, and I watched her cook. I watched her be a good example of a mother, especially the way she spent time with all of us, when we were small. The main thing was how she loved God and instilled the love of God in her kids. She was just a good Mother!

My Mom never had all types of men running in and out of our home. She was living for God and didn't play that. I may have done a lot in my life, but having different men over my kids, I never believed in that. Have I lived with a man without being married? Yes. But only two out of my whole life, and the first one became my husband.

I don't judge anyone that does that, and I've seen women who have a man this month, then he's gone, and here comes another one. That's not good for the children. Then, some kids start being molested right under their noses. Some women don't know, because they move man after man, into their homes, over their kids. Now, the children grow up and are very promiscuous. The mother doesn't know why and does not realize it's probably her fault.

With me being an adult now and thinking about incest within my family, the advice I would give a mother and father would be to guard your children, be very careful, and ask questions.

I was very overprotective of my daughter and watched everything. I know some parents may not do this, but I would always bathe her when she came back home from a weekend away. I would check her vagina to make sure it wasn't red or looked tampered with. I was just being a cautious mother. My daughter never had any issues that I could see and I'm very grateful for that.

CHAPTER 3

THE UNEXPECTED

It all started at a hangout spot with me and a friend. We were hanging out, and I was looking as pretty as ever. We were walking around the neighborhood and saw her cousin Tim, whom I knew. He approached me and said, "What's up girl?" I said, "Nothing," walking away blushing! Somehow, me and my friend ended up walking to his house. Tim had made it home and immediately, while standing there he said, "You so pretty," with a big smile. I said, "Thank you." He said, "Come here, ok? (nervously) come in my room." I didn't think nothing of it, so I said, "Ok!" Tim said, "You so pretty. You know I always wanted you." I said, "I didn't know that." Then he said, "Let me have you?" In my mind, I really didn't understand what that meant, but I instantly said, "You got a girlfriend." He responded, "No, I don't." So, we did a little talking, and of course, some lies took place.

Then surprisingly, at that moment, something took place that I didn't expect. I became impure. Becoming impure at that moment was not what I would have imagined. It was not what I've heard girls talk about. I didn't like losing my virginity to Tim. As a matter of fact, it was awful, not even worth my time. At that time, I didn't even know what love meant, nor did I understand about giving the most precious thing you have to someone, and not enjoying that moment. As I think back, as a woman now, I wish I had waited, because giving up something that precious is very meaningful. That experience with Tim was something I wished never happened. I wish I had experienced that with someone who really loved me, and would have cared enough to at least call me the next day, unlike Tim.

After that experience, I went on with life, but I think I did a little more than an average teen. I always looked older, even though I was just 15. I partied with older teens and young adults. We would go to what we called, 'the hole in the wall' clubs, house parties, and hang out spots. I had this one special friend, Kiya, that I just loved to be around. We would walk all day, because the neighborhood was the spot to be where we lived, and my family members were very popular. I loved that. It was always a party and hang out spot going on.

I was a pretty young thang, with a Coca-Cola shape. No problems at all in my mind. I was a bag of chips and everything else that was good. So, men were after me. I didn't know any better, I guess you could say I was young and dumb. There were men and teens, my age, always trying to get at me. I always thought if I said 'no' when they tried to holla, they wouldn't like me. Little did I know, they didn't like me no way, but as usual it was always, 'you so pretty; when are you gone let me get that?' I was thinking, O God, I'm just a piece of meat to these men. Now, when I think about it, all these boys and men had on their mind was sex and sex only.

Even some family members looked at me cross-eyed. Am I that fine, Lord? Imagine your uncle always looking at you, while rubbing his penis. Sometimes, I would just be in a room doing something or looking at TV, and I would look up and see him fondling himself in another room, and looking at me until he reached ejaculation. What kind of nasty mess is that??? Why would you even look at your niece in a sexual way? That's disturbing and nasty! Even back then it made me wonder, 'what is this on me that makes people just want my body?' I don't run up in these men's faces. Is it something on me that says, 'here I am, take me?'

I went on with life, and these men were still after me. My God, what is this? I got it, they just wanted my body. How can I say, no? How can I get them to leave me alone? I just wanted a boyfriend.

I just wanted to be loved and not feel mistreated or used. But it was always, 'You So Pretty!' I didn't lay with every man that came my way. I started saying to myself, 'It must be some talking going on because this is ridiculous.'

CHAPTER 4

FIRST LOVE

It was the summer of 1995, when I met Ja'mii. I do not recall how we met, but all I know is, I saw this cute, handsome guy. I knew who he was through close family friends, so he was not exactly a stranger. When I was a teen, I was always on a scene somewhere, so it was very easy to meet different people. I hung out with my older sister, and we were always somewhere riding around.

Me and Ja'mii hit it off good. At that time, he was the type of guy I was really into. I liked the guys who lived the fast lifestyle and were getting into the fast money. Ja'mii had his own money, of course, and he was about three years older than me, but I did not care. I was going to enjoy the lifestyle that I loved so much. Ja'mii always told me how pretty I was, so that always made me melt.

At these times in life, beepers were in; we did not have the luxury of a cell phone, like now-a-days. Every time I wanted to talk to Ja'mii, I would always just beep him, and if I wanted to talk real fast, I would put 911 on the end of the beep, about 10 times! LOL! That is so funny now!

My mom used to work a lot, so that gave me all the opportunity to sneak, and go riding with Ja'mii, or catch a cab to his house, before my mom got off work. After a while, me and Ja'mii got really close, and I was in love to the point where I didn't care if I got a whooping or not, for being involved with him. I knew I would get in trouble if my mom found out, because my mom didn't play the dating game.

I don't even remember her letting me date, at all. I just did what I wanted to do, because she was so strict.

Now let me tell you this, Ja'mii had a girlfriend that I eventually found out about, but it was to the point where he didn't care, and I surely didn't, because I was already head over heels, in love. Ja'mii used to be over her house every day, because they stayed right across the street from each other. But while he used to be over her house, he would call and talk to me, all the time. Of course, he would always say they weren't together as a couple, and the way my mindset was at the time, I wouldn't have cared. I was just so in love with him.

I knew her, too. She was someone I went to school with. Actually, we were good friends in elementary school. By now though, it was too late. I knew nothing about him and her, and to me, he was my man! He could have told me she was his pet monkey, and I would have believed him. That is just how in love I was with Ja'mii.

When I could not get in touch with Ja'mii, I would always call this business, that was next door to his house. I would ask the man on the other end, "Have you seen Ja'mii?" and he would say, "Yes, he's over that girl's house." Sometimes it would bother me, because I would try to figure out why he used to be over there all day and night. But Ja'mii would tell me, he was just using the phone to call me. Like I said, he could tell me anything and I would believe him.

Of course, Ja'mii and I became sexually active, after a while. So, to me, he was my man, for real. I never had any run-ins with the other female. I just wasn't that type to fuss with no woman over a man, that was going to keep on doing what he wanted to do, after the fuss was over, anyway. Why waste all that time fussing and fighting, knowing he's still going to lie to the both of us.

I would literally call the man at the business every day, and he would give me the scoop on what he was doing. Anyway, I had firsthand news and Ja'mii didn't even know it. He would just always try to figure out how I knew everything he was doing. I knew every night he didn't stay at home and when he did stay home. I knew when he was over her house throughout the day, everything, even down to him washing the car. Yes, I knew everything, so he couldn't lie about anything, even if I asked him.

That summer me and Ja'mii were always somewhere in the streets, riding. I was just in love with the thought of him having his own money and car, even though I worked as well.

He used to come to my job. I worked at a fast-food restaurant (my first job), and I made sure he had extra servings on his tray, every time he came to my job. My man was going to be full indeed.

Football season approached and I've never been a sports fan, but me and Ja'mii came up with this plan to go to the game, one Friday night, just to spend some time together. I asked my mom, could I go to the game Friday, and she said I could go. That week I talked to Ja'mii and told him I could go to the game, and I wanted him to pick me up. He had a drop top corvette, so I knew my hair was about to blow in the wind.

He came to pick me up and we rode around town a little bit. Then he said, "What you want to do, go with me or to the game?" My thought process was on high speed! Should I go or should I not? Should I go to the game and go home, or go with my man? He said, "Now if you go with me, I am not bringing you back tonight." My thought pattern was still on a high. I was thinking about my mom and that whooping I could possibly get or stay with my man and forget all about that whooping.

While we were riding, and that wind was blowing, and my thought pattern was on high, I looked over and told him, "my mom's going to beat my butt if I stay out all night." So, I kept looking at him long and hard. Then I told him, "MASH OUT! I'm going with you. Let's ride!" I was, as they said back then, 'bout it, bout it!' I didn't care about getting a whooping or the consequences. We bypassed that game and I was not even worried about it; I did not care. My thoughts were, I'm about to spend all night with my man!

So, we went to his uncle's house, in the country. I was like a child on Christmas morning. Never once did I think about my mom being worried about me, or if she would lose sleep over my not coming back home after the game. All I was thinking about was, I am going with my man. The things we do when we're young.

Of course, we got in bed and his first words were, "Are you worried about what your mom is going to do when you go home in the morning?" I told Ja'mii, "Yes! I already know I am going to get a whooping, but I don't care. We might as well make the best out of this night," and we did. The next morning came and when it was time to go, I told Ja'mii, "I know I am going to get a whooping, so, just take me home." We pulled up to a location across from my house, so no one could see me get out of his car. I kissed him and told him I loved him and went toward the house, as he pulled off. I walked down that hill, went in the house, and the first thing I heard was my baby sister say, "Momma told me to call her when you get here." I said, "You better not call her," but she did anyway, and boy was I scared.

My mom pulled up with the police. I was just in the living room. I already knew she was going to tear me up, so I was somewhat expecting the beat down. So, they came in the house, of course she asked me, "Where you been all night?" I was definitely not telling that information at all. As she and the police stood there, she said, "I am about to beat your tail, and the police going to say, 'go ahead Mrs., you have my permission.'" When I say she tore me up! Even though I was prepared for that whooping all night, I was screaming and running around that living room like crazy, and she was going to work on me!

Then after that, she went back to her job. Before leaving, she told me I better not go nowhere or get on the phone! I chewed my little sister up about calling my mom. I was fussing bad at her. She said, "I just did what momma told me to do." I was so mad with her. Honestly, at that point, I really did not care about the whooping I just had gotten. I just wanted to beat her up for telling I made it home.

After all that, I went and got in the bed and slept all day. I had a long night and a long morning, so I was tired and needed some rest (lol). Even though I got that whooping that morning, it still did not stop me from seeing Ja'mii. Now, thinking back all those years ago, I should have just gone home. That would have been the smart thing to do.

I spoke to my mom about that night in my adult years. She told me, she thought something had happened to me, and she couldn't sleep, because she didn't know if I was dead or alive. I feel bad now, but at the time, all I had on my mind was my man and the fact that I was so in love, to the point where I settled for lies and risking it all. My mom could have put me out, but she didn't. I'm just happy that she only whooped me and didn't send me to a juvenile facility!

The relationship with me and Ja'mii lasted a few years after that. I was still in love and still listening to the lies about the other girl. Eventually, I grew older and we just grew apart. Till this day, Ja'mii still tries to talk to me, but I look at him and laugh to myself now, and say, did I really go there? This is who I was in love with? This is who I got that beat down for??? With his lifestyle now, and how crazy in love I was with him then, I can truly say, "God, thank you for pulling me out of that." I know his wife has caught it. I can tell by his looks.

CHAPTER 5

PARTY LIFE

At the age of seventeen, I was old enough to work. So being rebellious towards my mother, I was put out, and went to stay with my grandmother. I knew I was about to party and do what I wanted to do now.

One weekend, I was partying, and I met this guy named Shun. He was cute and tall, with different colored eyes. I am mesmerized. Shun was older, in his early 30's. We hit it off instantly, and I thought I was a prize. No, no, no! Homeboy had a woman. I was stunned! I thought I was the one! I thought I was his girl! He was popular, so I put up with the mess, the women, and the fact that he was broke. After a while being with him, things started to change. I would call him, the person on the other end of the phone would always say, "Shun not here," but the car was there. I would call back to back and always lies, "He's not here." My response was, "Yes, he is, so why are you lying?" The person who was always lying to me, saying he is not here, was someone I loved, and would do anything in the world for her, but 'He's not here,' was a slap in my face. That's when I learned no matter how nice, or how sweet you are to your significant other's family, they'll still lie and protect that person, knowing that person is hurting and lying to you. They go right along with their mess.

So, now I was looking like a fool to these people, because I stayed even though he was the one playing games with me. I wanted people to know I was his pretty young thing. Yeah right, we didn't go anywhere until my payday. We went everywhere on my expense and I just couldn't wait until payday, because I was going to be with my man.

All week, up until my payday, he would be with his main woman, lying to me, and saying, "I'm not with her." But, I would always ride by her house and his car would be there, all the time. I would be so hurt on the inside.

I remember one night, I went out with his niece, and afterwards, I just wanted to go spend one night with him. After we left the club, I wanted to surprise him and be there when he got home. So, I went to his house and got in his bed; this was about 3 a.m. I got in the bed, all happy, and waiting anxiously, but to my surprise, he never even showed up. I guess after he left the club, he went over to another woman's house. I was so humiliated because he didn't come home. His mother figured out I was in there and asked me to leave. I was already hurt, and now embarrassed, too. I was so mad and heartbroken, but I went on with the mess he was giving for a while. Finally, I woke up, left that mentally abusive relationship, and realized Shun wasn't all that no way; teeth were fake, bald headed, and he definitely wasn't a bag of chips there, (you know where) either!

I moved on with my life but was still a little hurt. That did not stop me from partying, though. It was only then, a couple of family members and I partied like rock stars, every weekend. I worked through the week, but the weekends were dedicated and devoted to the clubs. I never just met men in the club and wanted relationships. I always thought, if he's in a club and partying with me, he won't be good for me, nor me good for him.

After the hurt decreased, I met this guy, Aren. From the beginning of the friendship, he bought me anything I wanted, but always wanted me in short dresses and my hair fixed. I liked him. I didn't have to prove my love with my check to Aren. We spent a lot of time together. We went out of town a lot, and he always gave me money, but the requirement was to always have on a short skirt. I felt good. I thought I was something, and had it going on. It was always 'you so pretty.'

We would go to Atlanta from time to time, to his cousin's house, who was an NFL football player. His house was so big and nice on the inside. I wasn't used to that, so I was completely in awe! Here's the twist, Aren had a girlfriend too, that I knew nothing about. I was like, 'O God!' Why do these men keep lying to me, to get me all wrapped up in them, and then I find out there is a whole, additional secret life. Of course, I confronted Aren. Same line as usual, "she's not my girlfriend. We just have a child together; it's not like that." And me, being dumb enough to believe it, to a certain extent. I stayed, because I liked Aren and he was treating me so nice. I loved our little getaways. Eventually, I just could not take the lies about the girlfriend anymore. So, I just left that relationship alone.

I'm older, eighteen; still considered a teen, but in my mind, I am grown. I moved out and got my own place. My mother bought my furniture and I thought I was living it up, until the bills started rolling in. My God! I needed help. Well, my mother stepped in and paid my rent, it was hard living on my own, but I wasn't a lazy person, so I would work. I had to work at my mom's business as a shampoo girl, because she helped me pay my bills. I enjoyed it, and didn't mind, because being in a salon was my passion. I love everything associated with Cosmetology and beauty, still up until this day. I would date here and there, but nothing serious.

I'm a great cook, and I take pride in knowing how to do that. It's something about feeding a person and putting a smile on their face. Even though I ended the relationship with Shun, he would still call from time to time, and of course, me being young and dumb, I would fall for his tricks. He would say, "I'm coming to spend the night with you." Man, I used to be so excited, because I was already bored, living by myself. The day came for him to spend the night, and he asked me, "Can you cook something?" My response was, "YES! That's no problem!" So, on that day I cooked a big meal. I was so excited!!

I called him, once I was finished cooking, and told him everything was ready. He said, "Ok, I'll be over in a little bit."

I didn't want to eat until Shun arrived, so I waited. An hour went by, no Shun. So, I called and he said, "I'm coming! I got a little busy, but I'm on the way." Another hour, then 2 more hours... By then I went ahead and fixed my plate to eat. Shun never showed up. I was hurt, because I felt like he could have been honest with me, instead of lying. He was the one who asked me to cook, I didn't initiate that. So, the lie was not called for. After that day, if he ever asked me to cook, I would never do it. I said the only way I would even cook something for him was if he was already at my house. I ended up having to throw most of that food away, because of the no show. It was the same old lies from our previous relationship and I wasn't about to deal with him on that level again. If I dealt with him it was on my terms and my time, not his.

I eventually moved back home with my mother. I was too young, it was hard, and I was very bored and lonely living by myself. I didn't like being back at home, because I had gotten a taste of living alone, and didn't have to deal with my baby brother and sister, but it was better than being lonely and worrying about bills.

CHAPTER 6

TRAPPED

A year went by and I had reached the age of 19. Then I met this guy Kylo. I thought, not my type, but he may treat me right. But, then how about he's already taken. He already has someone. Again, me being young and dumb and not caring, I think, I'm going to enjoy this. Little did my young mind know, I would be trapped. I would be caught up; I would be made a woman. I would change my entire life.

When I say trapped, not I 'couldn't get away' trapped, but meaning I never had this type of lifestyle, of being taken care of. So, I'm staying. I had my own house; although I never really stayed there, because I was just so caught up with Kylo. I was with him a lot! I was living life now and was loving it! I was getting what I never had, and I'm in it for the long haul, regardless of if he's got a woman who cares. In my mind, yeah, she got him, but he's really mine. I am all Kylo needs, and I'm going to please him like you can't. I'm going to do what you won't. I'm just going to take over. I'll respect you, and I won't argue with you. I won't even fuss when he's with you. Needless to say, I was young and dumb, again!!!

As this relationship went forward, I appeared to be happy, but in reality, I wasn't. I was always wondering and worrying about the other situation, with her. I think I'm this man's everything, but in reality, I'm not. Kylo's kisses made me weak, and it made me want to be with him more. I'm his princess, because I'm just so pretty. I'm the one satisfying Kylo's every need, and I'm the one with him, all the time. BOOM! No ma'am! You're not his princess. You're not the only one that can make him feel like no other. There are more! You're not the only one!!!

O God! Here we go again! Why doesn't this man want me? Why am I not his only? Well, I didn't care anymore. I'm staying. I'll just deal with knowing Kylo has other girlfriends. Was I scared? Yes! Scared of diseases, scared of being in the presence of these females, and not knowing who they were. I had invisible enemies, all because of a man. As time went by, even years, I grew tired. Tired of being mistreated, being used, and being made a fool of. Never was I just trying to be promiscuous; I just wanted love. But with love the way I handled it, my heart always ended up broken.

I always wondered why ugly girls or fat girls ended up with good men. How come any man, that was really good and decent, never came my way? What happened to, 'I'm so pretty?' Will I ever be worthy of being a trophy? Will I ever be the apple of a man's eye? "Am I ever going to be *the one?*" I got tired of questioning myself...

CHAPTER 7

GROWTH

I got pregnant when I was 20. Me and my baby's dad already knew each other. We went to school together, when we were in middle school. We used to sit beside each other in school. He used to crack jokes on kids all the time in school and would have me in tears. I used to talk to him on the phone, but as friends, talking about things that went on in school. His mom used to answer the phone and I thought she was so mean. I used to tell him, "Your mom is crazy." However, we still used to talk over the phone. I was 14 and he was 13, during that time.

When I was 14, my mom joined a new church. Before that, we weren't in church as much, like when we were kids. When we went to this church, my daughter's dad was a member there. So, I knew I would be laughing all week for sure, because he was just so silly. During our young years, we never came at each other in a relationship way, we were just young kids being friends. As crazy as this may sound, during that time, we were entering adulthood and one day we went to the church picnic. It was nothing to do at that moment because the food wasn't finished. So he said, "You want to leave and go riding for a minute?" I said, "Yeah." He said, "We'll come back." We left and ended up going to his house. One thing led to another and we became sexual. I was comfortable with him, because I had been knowing him all those years. I was shocked, but things happened, and that was an 'all of a sudden' thing. After that we went back to the picnic.

He wanted to come over to my house the next day, so I told him he could. I had my own place, so that wasn't a problem. We ended up being intimate again. About a month later, I was late for my cycle. It didn't bother me as much, because the birth control that I had previously been on would affect my cycle, so me being pregnant wasn't a thought. I took a test to be sure and it came up negative. I waited another week and took another one, and it was negative. I eventually went to the health department, took another test, and the nurse walked back in and said, "You are pregnant." I was so shocked, because I didn't think I could get pregnant. I was excited but after that, I started getting sick, the most awful feeling in the world! I was sick about 3 months, and after that I was fine. Her dad and I kept it a secret because we never told anyone that we even dealt with each other, on that level.

We would talk during the pregnancy, but nothing serious. We weren't in a relationship. While I was pregnant, I went back home with my mom again, because the smell in my house made me nauseous, due to my hormones changing. I stayed with my mom for a few months and moved back out when I was about 5 months. I applied for a housing project, so I would have somewhere to live that was based on income.

When I was 9 months, I was approved for a one-bedroom apartment. After about 3 weeks in the apartment, I went into labor. I felt a little kick and my water broke, at home. The pain of labor instantly started hurting my back. My oldest sister who was pregnant, too, lived around the corner and another friend of ours, was at my house in 5 minutes. I was in so much pain after my water broke. We made it to the hospital safely, even though she ran all the red lights, trying to get me there. When I got to the hospital, I went in through the emergency room. I was trying to stand up, but I couldn't. I felt the pain of labor, all in my legs 'till the point they were shaking. A nurse wheeled me up to labor and delivery, in a wheelchair. I was scared to get out of the chair and get on the bed, because of how my legs were shaking. I eventually got on the bed. Now, I was in full labor!

I didn't have an epidural; I chose natural birth. My sister, our friend who brought us to the hospital and my daddy, were in the room. Those pains were hitting me hard. I had pain in my back and it was a pain I never felt before. My dad came over to rub me in a comforting way, and I told him to get his hand off of me; don't touch me at all! That's how bad those pains were shooting up my back. I know he had good intentions, trying to help me and I wasn't trying to be mean; I was just hurting. My mom had just had surgery and was saying she couldn't come. I said, "Momma, you got to come! I never had a baby before." She decided to come, and I was so happy she did.

It was about 6 people in the room with me. The midwife said, "Ok, it's time to push." So, my sister was at the end of the bed, running back and forth, saying come on Disha! Come on Disha! That wasn't even the correct way to say her name. It's so funny now! She told me to push and I yelled, "I DON'T KNOW HOW!" She said, "Just push, as if you were having a bowel movement." I said, "I don't know how! My momma didn't teach me!" OMG! This is so funny, as I reflect back to that day. Finally, I pushed and my baby girl came. She was 7 pounds, 1 ounce. When she came, they brought her and laid her on my chest. I burst out and said, "Awwwwwww! She got hair!" She was the prettiest little thing I ever saw. I was in love.

After she was born, she developed pneumonia and had to be taken away to be treated. I breastfed, so the nurses would bring her back and forth, at feeding time. I had to go home when my 3 days were up, and I had to leave my baby. That was the hardest thing for me to do. I didn't have a car at the time, so I had to catch cabs back and forth. My stomach was very sore, and I didn't want to leave, so I asked the nurses if I could just sleep in the lobby. They said, "Ma'am we're going to give you a room to sleep in, don't worry." I was so happy, even though I couldn't see my baby. I was satisfied with that.

I was on the labor and delivery floor and she was on another side of the hospital, on the pediatric hall. The next day they admitted her in her own room, so I was able to stay with her, as her parent. My baby had an IV in her arm and that just killed me. I couldn't take it. Every day it would be a different IV somewhere. The last one they said they were going to have to stick it in her head. I cried like a baby. All I could think of was, my baby probably was in pain and the nurses were hurting her. We ended up being in the hospital 7 days before she was released to go home.

Once we were home, a nurse came out every day, twice a day, for 2 weeks, to give her antibiotics. She had an IV in her arm, so she could get the medicine. My house smelled like antibiotics the entire 2 weeks. Once the 2 weeks were up, she was never sick again, and went through her childhood; never getting sick again, unless it was a cold.

My daughter and I had some tough times. I lived in the housing projects for 5 years, in a one bedroom, so she slept with me until she was about 3. Then I got her a little toddler bed. Throughout raising her, I was without lights at points, put out of my home one time, and having to sometimes spend nights here and there, but I never let her go and live with anyone else. Where I went, she was always with me. I took raising my daughter very seriously and wasn't going to let anyone else raise her. When I struggled, she was going to be right with me, and if I had to sleep in my car, which I didn't ever get to that point, but if I had, she was going to be with me, as well.

I lived with a couple of people throughout my 20's, because I didn't understand the value of paying bills, but I would never live with people and didn't help. I always had a job; never been the type to freeload on anybody. I would always pay to stay where I lived, buy groceries, and most definitely, cook. I didn't care if the house was full of people, I would cook for everyone. I've never been the stingy type, either.

Once I reached 29, I became more stable and started understanding the value of paying rent. From then on, we were always in our own home, and didn't have to live with anyone else. Life as a mother has taught me valuable lessons. I learned regardless of any situation, don't give your children up, always pay your bills, and keep money, just in case you get in an emergency situation. Me and my daughter made it through a lot of storms and struggles, but it has made me the strong, independent woman I am today.

CHAPTER 8

AM I THE ONE?

Being a young mother to a daughter, my dream and goals were always to be an example to her, and to show her the way. Regardless of my wanting a relationship, I vowed never to have different men over her. I kept my promise to my daughter. She's considered a young adult now, and throughout her years on earth, I only lived with a man, twice.

When I was 23, I met Tre. He wasn't a stranger to me. We went to school together also, but I never looked at him in a relationship way. When we were in school, Tre had hair down his back, but he kept it in a ponytail. I used to ride the same school bus with him, but just used to mind my own business. After the years of us growing up, I didn't see Tre. I often wondered where he was. If I didn't see some of my classmates, I would think about where they were, and how their lives turned out.

One day I started a new job. I was so excited about this new job. My daughter was two at the time, so I had to do what I had to do, as a mother. During orientation, while signing my new hire paperwork, I looked up to see a familiar face. I couldn't really figure out if it was him or not, because his hair wasn't long, it was short and curly. I eventually asked him, "Isn't your name Tre?" He was like, "Yes." I said, "Do you remember me from school?" He said, "Yes." I asked him where he's been and told him that I had often wondered how he was doing, since middle school. He proceeded to tell me how his life turned out. We went into the orientation class and I was minding my business, listening to the person who was training us. When we had a break, he started talking to me again, and asked me for my number.

I told him to wait until after the class. Then, after the class, we were leaving and he ran behind me, trying to get my attention. He was smelling so good, he had me hypnotized. The scent just lingered, you could still smell him 10 minutes later!

As the day ended, I had to fulfill my motherly duties to my daughter. I went home to cook dinner for my daughter and was thinking about my new job. I heard the phone ring, and OMG, it was Tre! We talked about the usual things people talk about when first meeting. We got to know each other a little better. As we talked more, I liked what I was hearing, and I guess he liked what he was hearing, as well. We eventually became serious with each other, took things further, and began dating. Tre became a man that I fell so deeply in love with. In my mind, I wanted to live my life with Tre. I wanted to be his one and only. Me and Tre were spending so much time together, and he spent nights sometimes, but would leave because he would have to go to work. One day Mr. Tre said, he couldn't take it anymore. "I'm moving in," and he just moved his stuff in, then he said he wasn't leaving, and I didn't object. I was all for it. I was in heaven. Tre swept me off my feet. I finally felt I had a man that loved me. Now, I could walk with my head high, knowing he's mine, and coming home to me. I was so happy!

I was very respectful of my daughter. We never slept in the same bed, unless she wasn't home. I was very particular about what she saw and what was said around her. Tre didn't complain. He just wanted to make me happy. This new man in my life just felt so right; he was heaven sent. We had some good days and bad days, but I loved this man so much. He was the man who appeared to treat me like no other. My daughter loved Tre too. He treated her like his own. He bought things for her, and during the holidays, he would go above and beyond. When I had to work, he would watch her. I was nervous, but she loved him, so I knew he never did anything to harm her. I would be in the salon working. I needed the extra help and he was there.

CHAPTER 9

THE ENGAGEMENT

We started dating in May of 2003, started living together in June and in October, we were engaged. He proposed to me at my big momma's house, in front of a few family members. I cried with excitement and ecstatically said, "Yes!"

Things were going good between Tre and I. I started planning our wedding immediately. I already had a budget set, and I imagined a spring wedding with close family and friends. We started going to bridal shops picking out colors and getting everything together, and we were so happy; my daughter was, as well. We had arguments and disagreements, but that's normal in a relationship. For the most part, we were a happy couple.

We both were working, providing for our family, and spending a lot of time together. Tre was always there when I needed him, and he never had a problem doing anything for my daughter. He was perfect.

The following year, sadly and unfortunately, things didn't work out with Tre. It ended up being an abusive relationship. Things started happening where I saw signs that Tre was being dishonest, so I would just watch him to see if this was the right relationship for me. Tre and I had some very good times, and he was there for me every time I needed him, but he was a little jealous.

One night while Tre was in the shower, I prayed and asked God to show me if he was the one for me, and if this marriage was HIS will. I prayed, "Please show me", and it's like immediately, he showed me.

Tre got out of the shower and we got into a little argument. Then, I said some things he didn't like, he said things I didn't like, and it escalated. As I was arguing and walking off, he choked me from behind, to the point of me losing consciousness. My sister ended up coming to my house because she knew we were arguing. I called her prior to the argument getting heated and told her to come over. She told me, "No," but she was there when I was coming back to reality, after he choked me. I woke up coughing. She told me to go outside and get some air because I couldn't breathe. She didn't come to play either, she came prepared to get rid of Tre.

She was so mad with him and she often says, if she did not have kids, she would have cut him up that night; she had a knife in her bra. Well, I ended up going to the emergency room and was released. For about a week, my entire right side was numb from the choking, so I limped a little. I was so hurt! This was my fiancé, the man I was totally in love with. What was I going to do? With all this happening, should I leave, or should I stay? I didn't know which way to go. Did it happen because God was showing me what I prayed about; or did what happened, just happen, because we had a small argument? Do I put Tre out or do I let him stay? He hurt my heart and he shattered it in pieces. I loved this man so much. Lord help me!!

I put Tre out; I couldn't trust him anymore. He hurt me. Days went by and Tre kept calling saying, "I love you and I'm so deeply sorry. Please take me back." Sometimes he would say, "I want you to be my wife." I responded and told him I didn't know, because he hurt me and tried to take me out. I just didn't know.

Tre constantly called, so I said we could meet and talk about it. The meeting took place, and to be honest, I was so happy to be by him again. Remember, I was in love with this man. The meeting turned into, I'm coming back home; and me saying, "Ok baby."

As crazy as this sounds, I forgave him and I took him back, but things were never the same after that. I didn't trust him anymore.

I was hurt and on the real, I was scared. I took him back, because I loved him. Things went smooth, and Tre didn't try anything like that again. We went to church together, did family things and I was so happy, but I still kept my guard up. Tre was my heart. I adored this man, and I wanted a family with this man. Tre and I talked about it, and we decided to work on an additional family member, and also the wedding was still on.

As time progressed, almost a year into our relationship, Tre started doing little sneaky stuff. Tre started being a different person, and after a while, I just couldn't deal with it anymore. I ended up breaking up with him and putting him out again. He got his own place and I would go visit him, because I was still in love.

Finally, one day I told Tre, let's just move on. Tre wasn't trying to hear that. I was visiting him one day, sitting in my car. He was constantly saying, "Is it anyone else?" I would reply, "No," every time. I would explain to him that I just really wanted a closer relationship with God.

Tre didn't believe me, and we started arguing. I tried to pull off, but Tre would grab the steering wheel each time, until eventually I gave up trying to pull off. We were tussling, and somehow, I ended up out of the car. Tre jumped in my car and pulled off. My purse and everything, went with him. I was screaming for help; no one helped me at all. I called the police, but nobody came. I ended up walking home. Imagine walking home and your car keeps passing by you. I was so hurt.

Well, I finally made it home, and my car pulled up, but Tre wasn't in it. He had handed my car over to someone else that we knew, and they brought my car to me. My purse was in the car as well, but Tre stole all the money I just had worked hard for.

I was done with him at this point. Yes, I was in love, and yes, I wanted him, but not enough to keep going through this! I didn't take him back after that. I didn't care what went on with him after that. I was finished! We were over. It was time to leave this relationship alone and focus. So, I did just that.

It was not an easy break up. It was really traumatizing because he would be watching me from the bushes. I used to be scared to go in my house, alone. He would leave notes in my door that would say, "I saw you leaving today, and you so pretty." I was so scared he would catch me alone, run up behind me, and catch me off guard, and do something to me. Those were the most scary moments of my life, but he got into some trouble and ended up going to jail. On that night, I slept like a baby. I was no longer worried, no longer having to tell everyone who dropped me off to wait until I got into the house before leaving. Finally, my peace had come back.

After that relationship, I started getting my life back together. I still loved Tre, regardless of everything he did to hurt me. He still had a special place in my heart. No one else ever compared to him. Tre had his bad moments, but the good outweighed the bad. I carried him for years in my heart, and no one ever equaled to the good he did. No one was Tre. He stole my heart, but ripped it apart too. I had to get myself together and realize he was gone.

CHAPTER 10

THE FINAL STRAW

After Tre, I said, no more living together, because it affected my daughter. She just loved Tre so much. She was just a baby and didn't know what was going on.

Once again, years later, I wanted to love and be loved, so I tried another friendship. His name was Cody. After him trying to date me for about two years, I finally gave him a chance. We dated for a while and eventually lived together. I was miserable. There was no communication (period), not the way I would have liked it to be. He didn't like to talk and I'm a friendly person who loves to talk. So, that was a big issue for me. I remember us going on a date one time. I was so excited to get out of the house and have a nice outing, without the kids. We went to the movies, and afterwards a restaurant. Imagine walking in a restaurant, being seated, making your order, and seeing a crowd of people talking, laughing and having great fun, with their loved ones. But at your table the conversation is extra dry; no communication at all; just sitting there. I was saying to myself; this is a bunch of bull. We already didn't communicate like I thought we should have and now we have an outing with no talking. I was so disappointed and just wanted to go home.

Cody was a good person, helped around the house, went to work every day faithfully, but just lacked communication. I still stayed, because I wanted to know once again, "Am I the One?" Well, the answer was, "No!"

One night, Cody went out. I never had a problem with that. The club closes typically at 3 a.m. So, I woke up and it was five. Where's Cody? He wasn't there. I left that morning for church, and after church, when I arrived back home, his car was home. I wanted to fight, because he was ok. I wanted to fight because he never thought to call me. I wanted to sit everything he owned, outside. I wanted to just light this house up and beat the crap out of him. But, I'm so pretty!!!

Now I was humble, and I never let my thoughts show. I just went into the room, closed the door, and called a close friend. At the time, I was so filled with emotions and hurt! I eventually went on to sleep.

The next day, I talked to another friend about what took place that Saturday night. Her name was Bailey. As I was talking, I said, "Girl, Cody didn't come home Saturday night. I just don't know where he was." Bailey had me hold on while she checked something in her computer; she worked at a hotel. Then, she said, "Girl! His name is in my system!" I said, "What girl?" Bailey said, "Girl, he was here! OMG!" Honestly, I knew it! I just knew it! So, I began the questions, "Bailey????!!!!! What time did he get there?" Response, "Around 3:30 a.m." OMG! "Well, what time did he come to pay for the room?" She said, "About 2 p.m., that same day." Now, in my mind, this was premeditated and planned. He used my water and soap to bathe, as well as my electricity to get himself ready to go out. Cody did all this under my nose, and I was clueless. To this day, he never knew that I knew he stayed at a hotel that night. That was it; I was done! This is over!

I never gave Cody a reason to cheat, and I was faithful. I was a good woman who respected him and treated his kids with respect. When I say I was tired of thinking, 'Am I the One?' And hearing 'you so pretty,' from guys. OMG! I put him out and told him I was moving back with my mom. So, that ended, and I said to myself, I could not take this anymore! I was tired. I left that situation so quickly.

As time went on, my daughter and I went back home, with my mom. I said, no new relationships. I'd rather deal with someone from my past, because they were familiar. So, from then on, that's what happened. My mindset was, I don't care how I'm treated anymore. I don't care if I'm dogged out, I don't care, because I will never be the one for anybody, even though these men say I'm just so pretty.

Throughout the years, I went through a lot more in life. I've endured things I shouldn't have, and I put up with some things I should have never allowed. I put my self-esteem on the back burner, just to feel loved. I did it just to feel like someone cared; just to say I had someone. Did I mean anything to these men? In my mind, NOOOO! I was just something to do. I was just a toy. Will someone ever love me? Will someone ever care? Will it just always be, 'You so pretty?' Will I ever be the one? Will I ever be *the one*???

CHAPTER 11

MAD

I got a call and it's Hakim who says, "Let's hook up." Ok, I didn't have a problem with it, because he was a previous guy. I was bad about backtracking. I guess that's how I dealt with the issue of not wanting to be hurt by a new relationship. So, we hooked up. I was a fully grown, 28 years old, handling my business, but just got in a rough spot, to be honest. That's how the hook up even got hooked up.

So, we met up. Here I am, just thinking about what I came for. Thinking, let's get this over with, so I can get back to my usual. During the sexual mix, I was being cautious and asked him to let me make sure everything is still covered and protected; let me see! So, he showed me, and it was covered up.

At the ending point, Hakim jumped up and did a quick cover-up of himself, with his hands, down below. Then, he stared at me. I was like, OMG! something isn't right. What did you do that for??!! Then, I touched down there, and what I felt on my vagina, I didn't like!! Instantly I panicked and yelled, "What happened?" He answered, "I don't know." "What do you mean, you don't know?" Immediately I said, "Everything was still covered! I saw it and it was. Then you must have quickly taken off the protection you had on, without me knowing." I panicked in my head thinking, the unthinkable better not happen, and I better not get pregnant. I was furious with Hakim.

So, weeks went by and I was still wondering if I was pregnant. I was a wreck. I was already going through a rough time in my life, me and my daughter were now living with my mom. I spoke with my friend, Kae, at that time, and told her what happened. I told Kae I just knew Hakim took the protection off; it didn't just come off. I was so angry, and while we were conversing, I told her, I was going to call Hakim and just say I'm pregnant; just to get the truth out of him. Kae said, "Girl do it!" So, I called Hakim. He answered me, I was trying to be all sweet, but in reality, I was really livid.

The conversation went straight to the point. "I'm pregnant! Why did you do that? I made sure I protected myself, but you took it upon yourself to uncover without my knowledge." "Wonda, I'm sorry!"

Instantly I grew even angrier, but I had to keep playing the role over the phone, to get the truth out of him. I said, "What are we going to do, because you did this? You chose to uncover what I made sure was covered." Hakim said, "I'm going to help you." I Instantly ended that conversation because I was really furious.

I called Kae right back, "Girl, he did it. He uncovered himself without my knowledge." "Girl, I'm so mad!" I'm a female that knows my body. When I calculated back to the day, it was around the time I could conceive. OMG! I'm a wreck! So now, I'll just wait for Sally to appear, on her right date. I was not going to stress it.

Time went by, a week or so, and no Sally. OMG! I was getting furious in my mind, because I wanted to see Sally! Oh God, Sally is never late. She always comes on the correct day, no missing. Sally never showed, so now I'm ready to fight, because this wasn't in the plan. I took extra precautions to cover, and he uncovered without my knowledge. I have to deal with if I may be pregnant or not, while he's living his life. I bought a test, it was positive. Now, I was ready to just beat Hakim up. The next day, I went and bought another test; it was positive, again. I was saying in my mind, this is wrong, and I continued to buy tests. It was roughly four more tests that were positive. I was in denial. I was angry, and I felt like I was raped, by my decision to be protected, and

Hakim taking advantage of me, without my consent. I wanted to holler! I wanted to blow his house up, and I was still in denial. I made an appointment at a pregnancy center; tested positive, again. Oh, it's wrong. Well, I did not accept that I was pregnant until I went to my ob/gyn doctor, and a blood test was done. I was so hurt and disgusted. Maybe if I were not thinking about my rough spot, this wouldn't have happened. I cried so, so much, and I spoke to Kae about this every day. I cried every day, all day. I was already depressed, and then, here comes the morning sickness. I was extra angry and I was sick! I couldn't do anything, but work, and lay around. My hair was standing straight up on top of my head. I just didn't care, because I was mad and depressed.

I called Hakim and told him I was pregnant, for real. The last time I called, it was only for him to tell me what he did. I said, "Why did you do this? If this was what I wanted, I would have said no need to cover." He said, "Wonda, I'll help you."

I was always crying, now. Every day, I told myself I was not going to tell anybody, that I'm close to, about this pregnancy, because I was not going to have it.

I would call Hakim every day, mad and asking, "Why did you do this?" One day I said, I just hope you help with this baby. He said, "I'm not going to promise you that, I got other kids I have to take care of, and two graduating." OMG! That crushed me instantly. I felt like I didn't want this baby to be unloved by its dad, like my daughter felt unloved by her dad. I didn't want this baby to feel hurt, like my daughter is always feeling about her dad. I was doing all I could as a mother, but my daughter was feeling unloved and unwanted, by her other parent. I didn't want this baby to go through that. I was a wreck and so unstable in my mind. I was tired of Hakim changing his story and now telling me, he was not going to help. I was going to have to do this on my own.

I just wanted to die on the inside. Two kids feeling unloved, that crushed my heart. I did the unthinkable and called the abortion clinic. I got scared and decided I could not do this. Then, Hakim would call and still say, "If you have this baby, everything is on you. I'm not helping." I'm even more depressed now. I was already sick, couldn't eat, walking around looking like a zombie, but you did this to me, I was thinking.

I pondered over having the baby or not having the baby. Every time I got sick; I was angry. Every time I didn't have the energy, I was upset. I WAS JUST A MAD BLACK WOMAN!!! So, I went on about my regular schedule, working, coming home, crying every day. I was pondering on what I should do. Should I have this baby and struggle, or should I do away with it to make it better?

At the time my close friend Kae, and I would still talk every day and I'd cry. I'd say, "I just can't do it." Hakim was not going to love this baby, and he was not going to help me. I was just going to have an abortion. She said, "You sure?" I said, "Yes!" I was tired of crying, and tired of him telling me everything was on me. I was tired of being sick and depressed. She said, "I've had a few, you'll be fine." So, I called a clinic and made an appointment.

I started feeling better in my mind, because I knew everything was about to be over. At the time, I had a very good guy friend named Red, and he said, "Don't do it. I'll help you out with the baby." So, I said, "Ok." Red would tell me that I needed to tell my mom I was pregnant, or he was going to. I said, "Nooo! Please don't do that." I didn't want anybody to know.

He said, "Please have it." So, I agreed. I started to think positively every day, getting my strength up; still a little angry, but everything was looking clearer to me.

My mom got the call. She asked me about the pregnancy. I told her it was true, and she asked, "Who it was by?" I was not telling that part. My mind was made up. I'm having another baby. My daughter was seven at the time, so here's her playmate. I stopped calling Hakim because it would just upset me really bad.

One day I was talking to Red who encouraged me to have the baby. He asked how I was feeling, and I said, "Fine; just laying around." Then, I told him the truth, because I was not feeling good at all. I said, "I'm so tired of being sick, with no energy. I just hate this happened to me, and I didn't want this; that's why I protected myself." I started crying again. Then, he said, "Girl, you shouldn't have been over there, doing what you were doing; you wouldn't be pregnant. But, you did, so deal with it, because it's still your fault."

OMG! That hurt my feelings to the core. I said to myself, he's not going to help me like he said. I made an appointment. I went to the clinic and they did an ultrasound. The lady said, "Do you want to look?" I said, "No." I was very emotional and still undecided, but I was there now and my friend Kae was waiting for me in the lobby. I went through with the procedure, and I left there feeling like I hit the lottery. I wasn't sick or feeling bad anymore. I was normal again. I wanted to eat, and we went straight to a restaurant, where I pigged out. I had gotten my life back now and moving around, I felt 100% better. I moved back out on my own, so I was good.

Now that was in October. In January, towards the middle, I just started grieving and crying out of nowhere. Every day I felt convicted about what I did. That same year in April, I was at a wedding, doing fine. Me, my sisters, and my mom were sitting together at a table. I saw a pregnant woman and I instantly started crying. I ran out of the room. My mom and sisters said, "What's wrong with you?" I would always say, "Nothing."

Every time I would see a pregnant woman, I would just cry; tears would just flow. After the procedure, I felt like a million bucks, but little did I know grief and depression were coming after. I hated I did the procedure, and kept thinking, why didn't I have the baby? Why didn't I just get prayer? Why didn't I talk to positive people, that would encourage me? Why didn't I just cry out to God and depend on Him to lead me and guide me, with the baby? Why was I selfish and why didn't I just have the baby? Why? Why? Why? I grieved for an entire year after that procedure. I cried secretly every day for a year. I beat myself up and was mad with myself.

I was at church one day and ran out crying. I didn't know someone came out, right behind me. Sister Jane stood with me, hugged me, and let me cry it out. I told her everything that happened, from the beginning to the end. I also told her I was still angry with Hakim, and she said, "You have to forgive him." I said, "No! I'm not ready. He did something to me that I didn't ask for and I'm mad." Sister Jane said, "Forgive him, and then God will forgive you." We talked for the entire church service, in a closet full of stuff. It was just standing room in there. But when I came out of that closet, my depression and crying were over. I have not cried any more, from that day to this one.

I eventually forgave Hakim. I went to him and told him how I felt about what he did to me, and how he made me feel when he would say everything was on me. I let it out, and he said, "I am so sorry. I shouldn't have done that." I told Hakim, "Every time I see you, I cry, no matter where I am. I cry with grief for our child. You hurt me. You did something to me that I tried to avoid." I told Hakim, "Please don't do that to anyone else, because your decision really affected my life."
I have gone through almost two years of depression and grief, but I forgive you and accept your apology. After that day, my life changed.

I was back to myself. I prayed a specific prayer, one day, heading to church, "Lord, please forgive me for what I did. You blessed me with my second child, but me being selfish, I aborted the blessing, instead of raising the baby, like I did my daughter. I aborted this one. I'm so sorry God. I know I aborted the blessing, but please bless me with another child, one day. Don't take that away from me. I'll never do anything like that again and I'll tell anybody I know, who's contemplating abortion, not to do it, because it's not worth it." Six years later, I'm pregnant!!

CHAPTER 12

THE REMIX

Years went by, and because of what I've been through in life, it was easy for me, like I said, to go back to the familiar. After so many years of being away from Tre, we hooked back up after 9 years. I've always had love for Tre. I guess I held on to the good memories we shared but, boy there were some bad, awful memories as well. I forgave him for the things he did to me in the past and moved on with life. I dated here and there, after Tre, but always had Tre in the back of my mind, wishing he had done right. I would talk to him here and there, throughout the years, but nothing serious. I guess when the opportunity presented itself, we ended up back together.

We instantly went fast, because we were familiar. Tre stated, "I've missed you and we can work on a relationship." I agreed. I instantly said, "We're both grown, in our 30's, we know each other, have lived together, and know our likes and dislikes. Let's do this."

I laid the law down and I did not want to play anymore, or be hurt again by him, or any other man. Tre agreed to the new start. So, we met up. Tre said, "You so pretty and look the same." I was in a different place then and had been through a lot in life. I wasn't the same as the young woman I was, when we were in our early 20's. I had become a full, mature woman, that knew how to get it in the mud. So, I was excited to have Tre back in my life. I started thinking that Tre didn't have any kids when we were together, in our 20's. We tried but were not successful. So instantly, I asked Tre if he still wanted a child. I knew we were older, but I would still love to give him his first born and have my second.

I've never been the type of woman to want a lot of kids, especially not a lot of them by different men. That just wasn't my cup of tea. I would always say and think, 'I'm just too pretty for that' and my body wasn't made to have all those kids; or one day I may get married, have too many kids already, and couldn't give my husband any, because I had too many when I was younger. So, that was a 'No' for me. Not knocking anyone who has and does, but to each their own.

So, the plan went through to have a baby. Okay, we tried but weren't successful this go round, on the first month. So I said, "We'd just try next month," and Tre agreed. So I was determined to give the man I always had love for and cared for, a child. I was going to make sure he had his first. Yeah, we were older: I was 33 and he was 34.

I used to always tell him having no children at his age was good. He would always say he'd rather have his first with me, and I was all smiles! Well, the plans were made, so let's get rolling. We tried, and I meant I'm going to have this man's first. I've never been the one to want kids by someone who already had kids. I wanted to be the first mother to a man's child, so he would love the child differently. He would possibly have that different kind of love for me, and I didn't want drama from another baby's momma, about him. Now, that I'm thinking, I should have just had both of my kids by someone who had 20 kids, lol.

Tre and I tried on all the days that I could possibly conceive. We knew we would have to wait and see what would happen. The waiting game is not a joke. We both wanted to be excited, but wanted to wait. I had previous fertility issues that I took care of years prior, so I still didn't want to get my hopes up. Ok, now it's time for Sally. My breasts were extra sore, felt like someone beat me up with bricks. That's normal for a woman, when it's time for Sally, but not to the extent of how they were feeling.

We were talking over the phone, one day, I told Tre my breasts were unusually sore, and I said, "This could be a sign I'm pregnant." Tre wanted to be excited, but was like, "I do not want to get my hopes up." A week or two went by and no Sally. I told Tre, "She did not show up." I thought I'd give it a few more weeks. So, I went another week or so, and no Sally. I called and made an appointment with a pregnancy center, but I didn't tell Tre, because if I was, I wanted to surprise him. I made an appointment at a pregnancy center in Alabama, about ten minutes from where I lived.

I nervously went to my appointment, at the pregnancy center. When I arrived, I was thinking and really hoping I was pregnant. So, I went in the center and started looking at all the baby pamphlets on the shelves. The ladies in there were just smiling, while I was just nervous as ever. So, the lady who assisted me, asked me to come back to a room and I was still nervous, but hopeful it would be positive. She then asked me to go into the restroom, urinate in a cup, and leave it in the restroom. I went back into the room nervously, until the nurse came back in.

Then after about 15 minutes, she came back and said, "Miss Thomas, it's positive; you're pregnant!" OMG! The emotions, the tears, the gratefulness because I knew what I did 6 years prior. At that moment, I knew God honored my prayer, heard my cry, and had forgiven me. No, I wasn't married, as "they (the sanctimonious ones)," say you should be, but most of them weren't either; they just seem to have forgotten!

I went back home, so excited and ready to talk to Tre. He called and I told him I had something to tell him. With excitement, I said, "I went to the doctor today." He said, "Ok." I continued, "I took a test!" He said, "Please don't tell me you're not." I yelled, "I am! We're having a baby!" "OMG!" He cried! Then, I burst out and said, "I thought you couldn't have kids, because you're so old, lol!"

That day was so exciting for me. I couldn't wait to tell my daughter, I was pregnant. She was going to be a big sister, after 13 years of being the only child. When I told her, she was excited as well.

Time passed, about a week, and things got back to normal. Then came the morning sickness. "OMG!" I said, I wasn't ready for this. I was too old to go through this again. Yes, I was ready for another child, but forgot about the aftermath of being sick, no energy and moody. Now, I was mad because I was sick. I didn't even want to talk to Tre; just the thought of him, made me angry. He would call and I would say I don't want to talk. Poor Tre caught it from me. I broke up with him that quick, because my hormones were all over the place. I had a business I was trying to run, and I would go to work, but couldn't hardly work, from being so sick and nauseated; I was miserable.

Imagine trying to do clients' hair and just feeling awfully sick. That was the worst ever. I just wanted to go home and lay down. My sister who was a stylist in my salon, would say, "Girl, you need to get yourself together and get finished." What would normally take me an hour, was taking me 2-3 hours, because I had no energy and was very sick.

After a while, I just took myself out of work. I laid in bed all day, every day, was deathly hungry, but when I would eat, it came right back up. Smells would get to me, too. I just hated everything. I didn't want to talk to nobody, not even Tre. I just stayed in my little bubble, in my room, looking at Little House on The Prairie, Matlock and Murder She Wrote, every day, all day. This sickness was something I did not experience with the other pregnancies. It was awful!

I had one scare in the early months of pregnancy. I went to sleep, and woke up to seeing blood. I was about 2 months then. OMG! I was so scared. I went to the hospital so fast, but after taking different tests, the baby was fine. That was a serious scare for me and Tre.

After about 3 months, I started feeling better; still would vomit from time to time, but I felt way better. Only problem I had was when I would vomit, I would just urinate on myself (lol). It's funny now, but I would have a towel at all times. I knew when I started feeling sick to grab the towel, put it on me, like a pamper, and run to the bathroom. OMG! All my towels were being used up, so quickly, ha,ha,ha!

As time went by in my pregnancy, I couldn't get up off of the bed without holding on to my bedroom door handle. Rest in peace to that handle, lol. I limped the entire pregnancy. I was very sore in my private area. It hurt for the doctors to check me. I was thinking, what kind of baby is this? I just wanted it out; hurry up 9 months! I just hated being pregnant, because of all that was coming along with it.

Around Christmas that year, I felt fine. Went to a Christmas lunch, had my little lunch, and when it was time to go get my daughter from school, I proceeded to get up to leave. I started walking and could hardly move. I thought again, what's going on now? What should have taken 5 minutes to get to my car, took me 30 minutes. I could hardly walk because I was in so much pain. So I went to the E.R., and everything was fine. They told me the baby was just very low. I was almost 7 months, at that time.

So as time passed, I went through another episode, and the same thing happened again, when I was almost 8 months. I had to go to the emergency room again, and at this point, I wanted to just be admitted and just have the baby. Well, that didn't happen.

Once I got there, they sent me up to labor and delivery. I got prepped for the nurse to check me and they monitored the baby's heartbeat. It was fine.

My daughter was with me, so while I was waiting on the nurse, I told her, I wished they'd go ahead and take him. That would be the most exciting thing ever. I told her, "Mommy is just tired and ready to meet your brother."

When the nurse came back in the room, she was trying to check me. I thought she was a little rough, but she was doing her job. I'm a big grown woman, but I was crying because of the pain of her checking me. This time when I left the hospital, the problem was solved; it was a bladder infection.

I had limped almost 5 months, and now with the medicine she gave me, the soreness went away that caused me to limp. I could get up now, without holding on to the door. I could even walk right, and I was so happy now that the issue was solved.

CHAPTER 13

THE BLESSING

Now it's time to prepare for the birth of the baby. I was going to the doctor every week, still a little tender below. It was about over then, so I just dealt with it. As I went to the doctor, I was not dilating and I was wondering what was going on, at 37 weeks with my daughter, I was going into labor. I went to the doctor at 38 weeks, still not dilating. I started getting worried and nervous. I thought of every way possible to go into labor. My first thought was, I am going to walk this baby down. I was tired of being pregnant. It was March, my due month. I had gotten my baby off to school and I said I was going to walk. I walked so far, until I could not go any more, and actually, my sister ended up picking me up. I just could not go any more. It's so funny now! I was just tired of being pregnant. So I went home that night, bounced around on a ball, did squats, pushups, and guess what, it was all for nothing. NOTHING WORKED! I just had a sore body.

I really got worried then, because by this time, at 39 weeks, I was still not dilating. I got on the phone and called my aunt to ask her to pray, because something wasn't right. When she prays things move, things get in line, and you see God's hands move instantly. She was on the phone praying, and when she got finished, she was speaking into my life about what was going on. Then, she said, "Everything is going to be just fine."

I went to the doctor that same week, and I had dilated to a 2. I told my doctor I wanted to be induced. He asked if I was sure, and of course, I told him, I was very sure.

The doctor said this can happen or that, and I said this is what I want. So, I made the appointment for that following Friday. I was so excited this was finally about to be over. I did not tell my family I was going in to be induced, because people would always say, just let the baby come on its own. No one knew how tired I was; how my body could not take being pregnant any longer. I was just over it.

The day before delivery, I got cute; had my nails and toes done, and put everything in place. My baby is finally about to be here! Friday morning came, I had to be at the hospital at 5 a.m. Me and my baby were there on time!

I had a peanut butter and jelly sandwich before we went to the hospital, and I was so scared it was going to come back up, but it didn't. I went in and got admitted. I was the happiest person in the world. This pregnancy was finally about to be over!

So, my close friend came to support me; he left out for a while. Now it was time to be induced. The doctor came in to break my water, but it was so painful to touch my vaginal area, he said he couldn't do it, because of me tensing up. He said I would have to get an epidural, but I said no, because I did not want that. Then he said, "Well, no baby today." Oh, I changed my mind quickly then. I was scared, because I heard so many bad stories about epidurals. I went ahead and got the epidural, even though I was scared. I just wanted to have my baby.

Well, I got that part done and when the doctor checked me, I was numb enough to break my water, and so he proceeded. The nurses were so good to me; they held my hand throughout the entire process. It didn't take long after that, before it was time to deliver the baby.

I am about to speak on the birth of my child, that I never really spoke about publicly, just to certain family members. So, the nurses came in and they were monitoring the baby's heartbeat.

Everything seemed fine. It was just me and them, at this time, and I heard my baby's heartbeat, which was normal. I was just laying there, just patiently waiting for my baby's arrival, and suddenly, all the nurses started running in looking at the monitor, checking the baby's heartbeat. I was still calm, just happy the baby was coming.

Out of nowhere, my doctor came in and said, "We have to prep you for an emergency C-section!" I didn't get nervous or anything. They were saying the baby's heartbeat was going down. I was still very calm and not nervous. When I say they rushed me out of that room so fast, I didn't have time to think, talk or call any of my family. All I felt was my bed moving and them rushing me to an operating room. Once we got in the room, the nurse was assuring me that everything was going to be okay. She held my hand and comforted me, as if she was my mother. She was rubbing my hand and kept saying, everything is fine. Then she said, "I need you to count backwards from 100 -1." I do not even think I got to 98, before I was knocked out. After that I heard them saying, "Miss Thomas, wake up, wake up." I was kind of out of it, and they said, "Here's your baby." I was so out of it, I said, "There's two of them?" All I saw was two big, yellow babies, (lol). They laughed and said, "No, it's just one." They had to take the baby to be put in an incubator. I think I just went right back out for a few hours.

When I finally was able to keep my eyes open, I saw my older sister. She was furious with me. Her words were, "WONDA!!!!!!! I'M ANGRY WITH YOU!!!!" I'm laying there mumbling and she said, "How are you going to come out here, have this baby, and didn't tell us?" She said, "I want to fight you, hahaha." I tried to explain, but really could not get it out. I was still out of it, somewhat. I knew people were going to say, do not get induced, just let the baby come. I had a beautiful 9-pound baby boy.

Let me tell you about my baby and the reason for the emergency surgery. He was trying to come down, but as he was trying to make his entrance, the cord was wrapped around his neck. As he continued to still come out, the cord double wrapped around his neck, and it caused his heart rate to drop. It dropped to the point of his heart stopping. When he was delivered, he was born blue and deceased, but after the doctor and nurses worked on him, he was able to be brought back. He had a lot of issues, once he was born, I was so hurt. I could not see him for 7 hours after the delivery, so I really did not even know how he looked until that night.

We were in the hospital 9 days. While in there I was told my blood pressure was up. I told the nurse I didn't have blood pressure problems, and she said, "Well you have it now." I had to start taking medicine immediately. Now, while I was dealing with that, my baby was fighting with jaundice, his weight started dropping, he couldn't grip his bottle's nipple, and was already born deceased. How much can a mother take? I spoke with Tre and told him the baby was born. He wanted to know what time? I told him, and he said at that exact time, when the baby was entering the world, he was asleep, and just start feeling very sick. He woke up feeling like he was drowning and couldn't catch his breath. I was in awe, because at that moment, he felt what his son was going through, while trying to come into this world. That was so strange to me. God is so amazing! All the while I was in the hospital, my family was very supportive. My oldest sister had my daughter, and she was sure to bring her every day, after school. I missed her so much, and I wanted her there with me, but she was too young.

My aunt stayed one night, and let me tell you all, she went to sleep. I woke up and had to use the restroom. I had the baby in the bed with me, so I couldn't talk loud, because my stomach was sore too. I was just calling my aunt to come get the baby and help me up. She was dead to the world!

I had to figure out how to put the baby down and how I was going to slowly ease up, while I was still calling her. After about 15 minutes of trying to get out the bed, I finally was able to get up. So, I made it to the restroom, the baby was crying on the bed, I could hardly get up off the commode, and I was still calling her name; no answer. I finally got up off the commode and slowly made it back to the bed, struggled to get on the bed and pick up the baby.

After I finally was able to get comfortable, then I heard a voice saying, "You called me?" I quickly said, "You're too late. I've struggled to get up, go to the restroom, and get back in bed now." After that night she was fired; she couldn't come back (lol).

It was almost time to be released to go home. I was so excited to finally go home to my daughter! My family was there to support me every step of the way. I really could not do anything, due to the surgery, and my feet were swollen so big, that they looked like elephant's feet. I think that was due to the blood pressure problem. My son went through what he did, coming in this world, but after it was all said and done, he's a healthy beautiful 6-year-old, that absolutely is in love with his mother. When I think back 6 years ago, do I regret being induced? No, I do not. Do I regret not having my family there at the time of my son's birth? Yes, I do. I have always felt, if I had not made the choice to go ahead and be induced, my son would have died inside of me. I just thank God, even though I aborted my second blessing, he still blessed me with my 3rd. It was a hard-unusual pregnancy, but I thank God for his life.

Life went on, and soon everything went back to normal. Tre and I decided to mend things back together. When I was pregnant, I just did not want any parts of him. Life was finally as I had dreamed!!!!

CHAPTER 14

LESSONS & CONSEQUENCES

As I look back over my life, at the age I am now, I think about how I've been through molestation in my early years, and how I should have told a trusted adult. If you have experienced bad things like this, talk to someone you trust and get counseling or therapy, if you feel you need too.

I had also been through so many ups and downs, in relationships. All I ever wanted was love. I started going through things with relationships, at the age of 13. The lessons I've learned were, I should have listened to my mother when she would tell me I couldn't go anywhere, when she would say you just want to be grown, and you don't want to listen. My life would have been so much better if I had.

I would watch everyone else's relationship, but not my own. I was in a whirlwind. I wanted to be in the crowd. Every time something was going on, I wanted to be there. Every party, every hot spot. It was, I am there, front and center! I never cared to listen to my parents, because I felt I was grown, and could do what I wanted to do. The consequences behind being defiant and disobedient, led me down a path of nothing but hurt, pain, being used, and being lied to.

I've carried hurt for years and realized men will lie to you, just to get what they want. When it's over, they'll go to the next female and treat her the same, if she lets him. I always thought I meant more to them than I actually did. I was just something to do and something to play with.

My advice to you is to think before you jump. If you jump too fast, it may cause you years of pain and heartbreaks. My mother just wanted what was best for me, but I was so fast, I just couldn't hear at the time. I love my kids, but if I had not been so fast, I would have had better fathers for my kids, less stress for me, and less worry.

Even though I've been dogged and misused, I can still say I'm a strong female, that knows her worth and value now. If you don't do anything else, take the words of encouragement that I've written here, and apply them to your life.

I know I'm not just a pretty face and good sex partner. I'm a woman who is valuable and I know for myself that I am so pretty, inside and out. No one else has to tell me that. Be encouraged and take my life's journeys as a lesson and don't make the same kind of mistakes as I did.

By the way, I got married but was I the one??

Stay tuned!

YOU SO PRETTY

ABOUT THE AUTHOR

WONDA THOMAS

I'm just a little country girl from Georgia, that's been through a lot; more than any words could ever express. I did not know better or like it, at these different stages in my life, but now I know what I've been through wasn't for me. It was for somebody else. I have two kids that I adore, a little granddaughter that is my heart, and a grandson that's on the way. I know he is going to steal my heart all over again, as well.

YOU SO PRETTY

Made in the USA
Columbia, SC
20 March 2021